Islands

by Sheila Anderson

first step non-fiction

Lerner Books · London ·

What is an **island?**

It is a kind of **landform.**

An island is a piece of land
in the water.

It has water on all sides.

Islands are mountain tops
sticking up out of the water.

Some islands are **volcanoes.**

Some islands are in the
sea.

Others are in lakes.

There are islands in rivers
and **ponds.**

Boats can sail around them.

Animals live on islands.

Plants grow on islands.

People live on islands.

They catch fish in the water
around the islands.

There are many things to
do on an island.

Would you like to explore
an island?

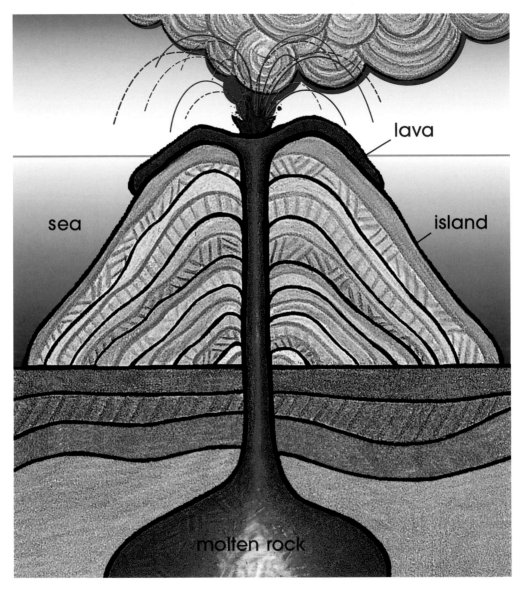

lava

sea

island

molten rock

Volcanic Islands

Some islands are formed when volcanoes erupt under the sea. Hot, molten (melted) rock from deep withIn the Earth comes out of a crack in the Earth's crust. It is pushed upwards. When the molten rock comes out it is called lava. The lava cools and makes a bump of new rock. More lava comes out and the bump gets bigger and bigger. It becomes an underwater mountain. When the mountain gets so tall that it sticks up out of the sea, it is an island.

Island Facts

 Many islands are formed when volcanoes erupt under the sea.

 The Hawaiian Islands are a group of volcanic islands. They are part of the USA.

 Japan is a country in Asia. It is made up of four main islands and more than three thousand smaller islands.

 The largest island in the world is Greenland. It is about nine times the size of the United Kingdom. More than half of Greenland is covered in ice.

 Many kinds of animals live on the Galapagos Islands in the Pacific Ocean. One of these is the giant tortoise. It can weigh more than 200 kilograms and can live for over 150 years!

Glossary

 island – a piece of land that has water on all sides

 landform – a natural feature of the Earth's surface

 ponds – bodies of water that are smaller than lakes

 sea - a large area of salt water that covers nearly three quarters of the Earth

 volcanoes – breaks in the Earth's surface where hot, molten (melted) rock called lava flows out

Index

The images in this book are used with the permission of: © Jason Hosking/Stone/Getty Images, pp 2, 22 (top); © Gary Yeowell/Photographer's Choice/Getty Images, pp 3, 22 (second from top); © Caroline von Tuempling/Stone/Getty Images, p 4; © istockphoto.com/Matthew Dixon, p 5; © Dick Roberts/Visuals Unlimited, p 6; © SuperStock, Inc./SuperStock, pp 7, 22 (bottom); © Wolcott Henry/National Geographic/Getty Images, pp 8, 22 (centre); © Chip Forelli/The Image Bank/Getty Images, p 10; © istockphoto.com/Ross Williamson, p 9; © age fotostock/SuperStock, p 11; © Joel Sartore/National Geographic/Getty Images, p 12; © Michael Cogliantry/Photonica/ Getty Images, p 13; © Wayne Walton/Lonely Planet Images/Getty Images, p 14; © Colin Prior/ Stone/Getty Images, p 15; © Kurt Scholz/SuperStock, p 16; © David Deas/DK Stock/Getty Images, p 17.

Front cover: © Henry Lehn/Visuals Unlimited.

First published in the United Kingdom in 2010 by
Lerner Books,
Dalton House,
60 Windsor Avenue,
London SW19 2RR

Website address: www.lernerbooks.co.uk

This edition was updated and edited for UK publication by Discovery Books Ltd.,
First Floor, 2 College Street, Ludlow, Shropshire SY8 1AN

British Library Cataloguing in Publication Data

Anderson, Sheila
Islands. - 2nd ed. - (First step nonfiction. Landforms)
1. Islands - Juvenile literature 2. Island ecology -
Juvenile literature
I. Title
551.4'2

ISBN-13: 978 0 7613 4366 0

Printed in China

First published in the United States of America in 2008
Text copyright © 2008 by Lerner Publishing Group, Inc.